The Good Mind

by Edgar Dale

Library of Congress Catalog Card Number: 78-50361
ISBN 0-87367-105-8
Copyright © 1978 by The Phi Delta Kappa Educational Foundation
Bloomington, Indiana

TABLE OF CONTENTS

What Is a Good Mind?

What is a mind, a good mind? John Dewey has defined it well: "Mind as a concrete thing is precisely the power to understand things in terms of the use made of them" (*Democracy and Education*, p. 39). He also says,

> To have a mind to do a thing is to foresee a future possibility; it is to have a plan for its accomplishment; it is to note the means which make the plan capable of execution and the obstructions in the way—or, if it is really a *mind* to do the thing and not a vague aspiration, it is to have a plan which takes account of resources and difficulties.

> Mind is capacity to refer present conditions to future results.... A man is stupid or blind or unintelligent—lacking in mind—just in the degree in which in any activity he does not know what he is about, namely, the probable consequences of his acts. (pp. 120-121)

A good mind must therefore be able to distinguish fact from fiction, truth from falsehood, the credible from the noncredible. Indeed, the term credence or credibility is a critical one in developing a good mind. If we study the works of able writers, especially able journalists, we realize that they are searchers for truth. To search means to observe carefully, to notice, to pay attention. A search may be for the presence or absence of something. To search then is more than mere inquiry; it is inquiry dominated by a penetrating view, a thoughtful concern.

A search means an exploration. Hence, the difference between a rigorous search and a mere inquiry is that the search will seek definite things. A search carries with it the idea of examining carefully, penetratingly, keenly, sharply.

7

The Questioning Mind

A penetrating mind, a questioning mind, is one that is not satisfied with quick, easy answers. The thinker does not give up quickly. When a search is going forward some ideas are usually in doubt or dispute. The search may be a way to find data on various aspects of that dispute. It is a questioning process.

There is a difference between the idea of asking a question and questioning. We do use the expression "to ask a question." But we can also have a questioning mood. It means a more determined search for the data, a more determined search for "answers" to the question under study.

A good mind is a questioning mind, a discerning mind. A good mind answers questions and questions answers. To have a question is to have a sense of doubt, a spirit of inquiry, a suggestion for further study, a feeling of needed continuity. A good mind does not accept finality nor does it assume that everything is in flux.

The good mind has developed the art of questioning. This approach to a liberal education has had a long and honorable history. Socrates, a great teacher who failed to publish, asked questions of his students and then questioned their answers. His reward was death by hemlock. Plutarch said, almost 2,000 years ago, "The man who wishes to make a careful answer must wait to apprehend exactly the sense and the intent of him who asks the question." Some members of television panels have not yet learned to do this.

John Stuart Mill, in his inaugural address as Rector of St. Andrews University in 1867, stated that we must "question all things, ... accept no doctrine either from ourselves or from other people without a rigid scrutiny by negative criticism; letting no fallacy, or incoherence, or confusion of thought step by unperceived." Do our colleges commonly follow Mill's advice of 100 years ago? Do professors encourage students to question all things, do they invite rigid scrutiny by negative criticism?

In "The Art of Questioning" in *The Teacher's Mentor*, Joshua G. Firch wrote, " . . . the whole sum of what may be said about questioning is comprised in this: It ought to set the learners thinking, to promote activity and energy on their parts, and to arouse the whole mental faculty into action, instead of blindly cultivating the memory at the expense of the higher intellectual powers." Do we follow this advice given in 1880, or are we still cultivating the memory at the expense of the higher intellectual powers?

We live in an answer-oriented world. Schools and colleges do not usually teach the art of questioning, but expect students to develop skill in answering questions that they didn't ask. We need to help students ask better questions—more profound, more provocative, more worthy of study.

When Gertrude Stein, who certainly had a good mind, lay dying she called to her companion, Alice B. Toklas, and said, "What is the answer?" Miss Toklas replied, "I don't know." Miss Stein said weakly, "Then what is the question?"

Those whose ambition is to have a good mind face three kinds of questions in and out of school: First, the big, perennial, open-ended questions that are concerned with the destiny, the ends, of men. The answers to these questions involve us in a continuing debate. Even the answers must be followed with a question mark. Second, there are the middle-sized, means-ends questions. There are good answers to these questions, but we should put a semicolon after the answers to show that they may not be final. Third, there are the little but important questions of means only, of finding answers to specific questions of limited scope. We can conclude these answers with a period.

The good mind is concerned with both little questions and big ones. The big questions are existential: "Who am I? What am I here for? Am I indispensable?" These are questions of identity, of purpose, of life direction. I once heard a minister say that no man is indispensable. But unless *all* men are indispensable, we must ask, "Who is dispensable and who sets up the standards for dispensability?" Nothing corrodes the human spirit so much as the feeling that nobody really cares, that we *are* dispensable.

The person striving to develop a good mind asks: What knowledge is of most worth? This perennial, big question has been raised by many philosophers and specifically by Herbert Spencer. I assume that the knowledge of most worth is knowledge of self, getting answers to the important questions noted above. The malaise, the disquietude, of today involves a confusion regarding acceptable roles. "How can I be a good son if I feel deeply that my parents' views on race or war are morally wrong?" "Is winning really so important? When you do win, what will you do with your winnings?"

Another big question: How does the good mind learn to communicate clearly, simply, parsimoniously? If we define communication as the sharing of ideas and feelings in a mood of mutuality, then we have a standard for performance. Is it true, as dramatist Tennessee Williams has said, that "men pity and love each other more deeply than they permit themselves to know"? If so, the great revolution ahead is not technological but a revolution in the hearts of men, in their empathy and compassion. More perhaps than we realize, we have steeled our hearts and minds against sharing with and caring for others. Many have become sophisticated, uninvolved spectators, have avoided participating in "the action and passion of our times."

Is our chief concern to help students become warmer, friendlier, more compassionate? Is study of the humanities aimed at making students more humane? Or do we see a good student as one who memorizes well, a bad student as one who memorizes badly? To suggest that gaining knowledge is the *chief* business of the school and that developing values is someone else's business is to abdicate responsibility for the education that makes knowledge fruitful, not dangerous. It puts the goal of a good mind in jeopardy.

A middle-sized question may deal with life management. We ask, "How do I learn how to learn? What is the most effective way for me to learn to read and write, to speak and listen, to visualize and observe?

10

How can I motivate myself to learn?

We must also ask and get answers to such critical management questions as, "How do I find the time, the energy, and the money to do what is important?" How do I find time to work with the League of Women Voters, the urban coalition, the church? How do I find time to read books? How do I create and conserve the energy required to work at my optimum? How do I learn to manage my money so that my money doesn't manage me? The good mind finds time to do the important.

Finally, there are the small questions, "Where can I find . . . ? Where do you look for . . . ? What does such-and-such a formula mean? How do you get to San Francisco from here? Who said, 'Punctuality is the thief of time'? Can I take a correspondence course in locksmithing? (Yes, you can.) What's the weather forecast? What's the difference between a thesaurus and a brontosaurus? Are these words correctly spelled: liaison, anoint, consensus, Ludwig Van Beethoven, innocuous, inoculate? Is it legal in my state for a man to marry his widow's sister? (The answer is, No, it's impossible.) Is it true that Alaska is the state farthest north, east, and west? Is a bat the only flying mammal? Does it nurse its young? What does *canst* mean?"

In a school or college dedicated to the methods of inquiry, what is the role of the teacher? The teacher's task is not to answer the big, medium-sized, and little questions, but rather to help students learn *how* to find the answers.

Answers are derived from three sources: first, one's own memory bank. Students must learn how to systematize the contents of their own minds so that retrieval is easy and efficient. Further, this systematized knowledge generates new knowledge. A good mind can be a storehouse of facts, but only as long as the stored facts are relevant and retrievable.

Second, there are other memory banks that should be at our fingertips. I refer to dictionaries of many kinds, yearbooks, the yellow pages of the phone book, encyclopedias, thesauri, atlases, gazeteers, and the like. Many answers to both big and little questions can be found in these sources. Every person who wants a good mind should have adequate reference materials within easy reach. The farther you must walk or ride to find answers to factual questions the less likely you are to do

11

it. *Availability* is a key component of all learning experience.

Third, computers can now provide increasingly easy access to the world's best answers to many kinds of questions. Computers can help us diagnose our present competencies— in vocabulary, the sciences, literature, foreign languages, investment, statistics—and provide the bibliographies or actual materials from automated libraries to remedy our weaknesses.

But do we encourage the development of the questioning mind? Why is it so hard to change the school and college from a place where the student memorizes answers to one where he raises questions and works independently to find the answers? Why do we continue to spend our time and energy on the lower mental processes of memorizing, and neglect the higher mental processes of critical questioning, of evaluation and application? These are the province of the good mind.

Many teachers have not themselves been exposed to thoughtful instructors who asked thoughtful questions that required thoughtful answers. Many students are not taught to read material with questions in mind and in a critical, questioning spirit. How often did an instructor present you with a list of "big" questions at the beginning of a course and require you to find "answers" to those that related to your needs? Some years ago Franklin Bobbitt gave his curriculum class at the University of Chicago such a list of questions, and I can still remember this baffling one: "Who is responsible for the education of a child?" The good mind grows by facing the challenge of "big" questions.

It may well be, too, that we have institutionalized a method of instruction that puts a premium on memorization and is antithetical to questioning. The little questions that have little answers are easy to grade. The big questions with varied and complex answers do not neatly fit a grading pattern. Further, the inquiry method puts a responsibility on the teacher, who may not be willing or able to accept it.

We may feel secure in a classroom as long as we are asking the questions, but we become anxious and uneasy when put on the spot by the puzzling questions of students. The chief role of a teacher is not to answer every question; it is to help students learn how to find the answers by themselves.

Thornton Wilder pointed out in *The Eighth Day* that "There is no true education save in answer to urgent questioning. Unease and deprivation awaken the young mind to inquiry. Roger did not realize that he and his sisters had acquired that habit of mind in their earliest years: They had struggled to survive. Like plants in a parched soil, they had sent down deep roots. From infancy they had groped hither and thither asking 'what?' and 'why?' and 'how?'"

Students and others will not develop good minds unless they keep asking "what?" "why?" and "how?" and then are encouraged and assisted to find good answers to their questions. Do you question this?

A Good Mind Is a Conceptualizing Mind

A good mind is aware that learning is a process of developing and refining concepts, applying them to old and new situations. A concept is a generalized idea about a class of objects or events. It deals with our experiences—tangible or intangible, concrete or abstract. To master a subject matter field is to learn its key concepts. These concepts include not only technical terms but also principles or generalizations. A concept may be a word, a principle, or a combination of the two. A concept may be limited or it may be overarching, a basic design for learning.

Some concepts are readily mastered—the 3,000 or so words that children bring with them to the first grade. Others are developed with ingredients that only age or mature reflection can provide, e.g., justice, love, responsibility. In all concept development there is a process of distillation, a moving from imprecision to precision. Concepts may be denotative, with high fences around them, or connotative, rich with associations.

Concepts may be verbal or nonverbal. Some have a name; others do not. We can think about textures, colors, images, tones, rhythms, without naming them. In face-to-face communication a raised eyebrow, a questioning look, or silence may convey far more than a spoken word. The earliest experiences of infancy are not verbalized—hot/cold, wet/dry, hungry/full. Mature experiences, however, include complicated mathematical, philosophical, or scientific concepts, expressed either as principles or as single terms.

A good mind knows when to put a verbal label on an experience. We like to give names to persons, things, or events so that we can put everything in its "proper" place, verbally conceptualize it. For example, we may label a person as liberal or conservative, a Catholic or a

Protestant, as able or inept. There is a real hazard, however, in premature labeling, thus freezing the name as final, conclusive, definitive. The Greeks used the word *atom* meaning *without cutting, indivisible.* But the atom was divisible—fissionable as well as fusible.

Labels are sometimes libels. They can't say, "Yes, but—" or "Handle with care!" People are liberal in some matters, conservative in others. Catholicism is changing, as is Protestantism. The convenient label may become an unexamined stereotype and concepts may suffer from hardening of the categories. Philosopher Alfred North Whitehead said, "At this moment scientists and skeptics are the leading dogmatists. Advance in detail is admitted; fundamental novelty is barred."

We can press too hard for labeling all concepts. Some of our richest experiences cannot be clearly labeled, easily classified, or transferred to others. They are uniquely personal, inexpressible, ineffable. Furthermore, meanings that are rich and evocative to some touch others only lightly. When artists paint, poets write, or sculptors carve or model, they may only partly express what they intended to say. There is, in William James's term, "an unclassified residuum."

A good mind knows the most effective ways to develop concepts, realizes the necessary stages through which most concepts develop. I see three major categories that can be identified on the scale from concrete to abstract.

First, we have the overt, concrete event itself in all its rich sensory appeal. It may be seen, handled, heard, tasted, smelled. It contains the rich juices of life, not yet dried up. It is firsthand experience, not secondhand or thirdhand. It involves little or no symbolism.

Second, as we move along the concrete/abstract scale, many experiences are *re*-presentations of firsthand experiences—condensed somewhat, rearranged, but still recognizable as directly related to the original thing or event. A photograph or a moving picture, a model, a simulation, a dramatization, a painting—all are semiconcrete experiences.

Finally, on the scale from concrete to abstract we come to experiences so fully condensed, so changed, that they no longer resemble the concrete or semiconcrete experience in any way. They have been "desensed." We have moved then from the event to the sign, and finally to the symbol. They have become representative, not *re*-presentative.

Why are the good mind and concept building so important to the teacher? The great hazard of all teaching is a premature emphasis on abstraction before the learner is "concretely" ready for it. Walt Whitman has good advice for us here: "[Language is] not an abstraction of the learn'd nor of dictionary-makers, but it is something arising out of the works, deeds, ties, joys, affections, tastes of long generations of humanity, and has its bases broad and low, close to the ground."

In too many textbooks the richly evocative concrete examples have been eliminated, and the learner is left either with a summary or a juiceless summary of a summary. A century and a half of world history may be described in a page and a half.

Teachers with good minds know how to diversify the experiences of learners, bridge the gap between concrete and abstract experiences. They can help the learners organize experiences and can provide additional experiences. But they cannot directly provide the "works, deeds, ties, joys, affections, tastes of long generations of humanity," and "its bases broad and low, close to the ground."

If the development of an integrated set of concepts in varied subject matter fields is so important, what must we do in schools and colleges to develop good minds? There are five things we can do:

First, we can teach concepts better by reducing the number we try to teach. We try too hard to cover the ground. Instead we should uncover it, teach in depth, not superficially.

Second, we must travel the route to conceptual depth through rich, firsthand experience. No one would assume that he could master the concept "Chinese food" unless he had tasted many different Chinese dishes. One cannot develop taste in reading except by savoring a variety of books and magazines, and reflecting on their meaning. Carefully selected television and film programs can furnish semiconcrete experiences needed for concept development. The television program "Roots," based on the book of the same name by Alex Haley, is an example.

Third, when the poet Horace suggested that we should "instruct with delight," he gave us a prime rule for mastering concepts. The root meaning of *delight* is "to charm" and "to entice." Some delight may come through self-discovery, figuring things out for oneself. I don't believe you need to discover personally everything you learn, but self-discovered knowledge does have a delightful flavor.

Fourth, a good mind not only masters key concepts but applies them daily. If we don't use our learning, we lose it. To develop high-level concepts we must constantly use them in the higher mental processes: inferring, analyzing, translating, applying, paraphrasing, interpreting, synthesizing, judging. The chief difference between the higher and the lower mental processes is that the lower mental processes usually involve retrieving unchanged ideas from our mental filing system. One's approach to concept development will differ markedly, depending on whether he is educating students or training them.

Fifth, we must list the critical terms and principles that we wish to teach and arrange them according to the level of mental processes they require. There should be national inventories on how well these concepts and principles are known, grade by grade, and then the concepts should be taught systematically on the basis of a carefully formulated educational design. It can be done. The writer, in cooperation with Joseph O'Rourke, has prepared a book titled *The Living Word Vocabulary*. It lists familiarity scores on more than 43,000 words, starting with *aardvark* and ending with *zymurgy*.

Every school should have an instructional resource center that could make available certain concrete, semiconcrete, or symbolic materials of instruction to help teach the desired concepts. The resource center would include facilities for drawing, painting, construction, measuring, dramatizing; and it would store plans for the use of local resources. It would offer a wide variety of reading materials, simulations, exhibits, films, and recordings.

In thinking about the mastery of concepts in developing the good mind we must not forget the most important concept of all, self-concept. Is the image in our personal mirror one of pride or of rejection? Have most people learned to test their full powers, learned to work to the limits of their capacity? Since most people do not use more than 50 to 60% of their potential, they should be able to increase sharply the quality and quantity of their concepts, read markedly better, use their time less wastefully, improve the quality of their human relations.

17

With these goals in mind, can we now conceptualize a revolutionary change in the schools, wherein we study everyone's present learning capacity, diagnose conceptual development, and help set up a learning program in which accomplishment will match potential? It would be well worth trying. It would produce a good mind.

Listening and Learning

Persons with good minds can communicate effectively. They can read and write, speak and listen, visualize and observe. They can send and receive ideas, produce, and consume.

Although these abilities are related, they do have distinct differences. We may read and write well but lack skill in visualizing and observing. We may lack skill in "picturing," creating images such as graphs, charts, photographs, cartoons, exhibits, and videotapes, despite the fact that we read well. A person with a good mind is a skillful observer; he or she notices. The person with a good mind is also a good listener.

To improve communication, to develop a good mind, we must see and hear language in all its richness. Language is a distillate of experience. Language is spoken and listened to. Language is written or pictured, and then read. We put meaning into what we hear as well as get meaning out of what we hear.

Reading and writing are two parts of a single process. Speaking and listening may be similarly described. We visualize by pictures, films, charts, or maps, and a good visualizer is a good observer. Reading, writing, visualizing, observing, speaking, and listening are essential parts of the language process.

The person with a good mind is a thoughtful listener. One must listen attentively to hear what is said, just as one must read to discover what the writer said. One must hear the lines. But one must also hear *between* the lines, catch the mood and intent of the speaker. One must judge the speaker's objectivity, his flexibility, and his adaptability. Is the speaker trying to *think* things over, or to *put* things over?

The listener must also go *beyond* the words that he hears. The listener must ask, "What does this mean to me as a person, or as a citizen, or as a parent? What are the implications for action?"

This means critical, discriminating listening. It means a willingness to examine points of view in our own thinking that we may have previously been unwilling to scrutinize. It is no secret that most of us listen chiefly to points of view with which we agree. We may be willing to rearrange our prejudices slightly, but not to examine them rigorously.

Good reading makes good conversation. Good conversation makes good listening. And good listening may stimulate a desire for good reading. No matter where you start in developing good communication skills, you will need to pay attention to these six aspects—writing/reading, speaking/listening, visualizing/observing.

Listening must be wholehearted as well as whole-minded. Listeners must do more than reproduce what has been said. They have an obligation to re-create it, to reconstruct, to sense its meaning for themselves, to make it an integral part of their thinking and action, not an unabsorbed addendum.

A good listener is usually a good reader, and vice versa. The late Paul McKee pointed out in *The Teaching of Reading in the Elementary School* that "In general, beyond the third grade level, the pupil who does not understand a statement which he attempts to read does not understand that statement when it is read or spoken to him. Furthermore, available data show that most pupils at intermediate and upper grade levels have as much difficulty in understanding the instructional talking of the teacher as they have in understanding what their textbooks say."

Reading and listening have advantages and disadvantages as media of communication. In listening to a person who is physically or visually present, as in television, we get a total impression—voice, mannerisms, apparent sincerity. This halo of reality may be lost in reading.

Listening, however, may sometimes be a very inadequate way to get meaning. If you miss a point in your reading, you can re-read. If you wish to linger over it, you can do so. You set your own pace. But you can't re-listen unless you have a recording or unless you can re-show the film and listen again to the sound track. Even if you have the recording, it may be troublesome to replay it for this purpose. And in radio broadcasts you may miss things that you wouldn't miss in face-to-face contact, either personally or on television. All of us are aided by reading the lips of a person who is speaking.

Why don't we listen? We don't listen because speakers do not suggest what we might do about the problem they have discussed. True, their major responsibility may be to define the problem. But out of their wisdom they should also help the audience define some possible responses, some hunches about possible action. Omar Khayyam had the same problem:

> Myself when young did eagerly frequent
> Doctor and Saint, and heard great argument
> About it and about: but evermore
> Came out by the same Door as in I went.

We don't listen because the speaker's words are too abstract, cold, un-evocative, and ill-chosen. Words can dazzle without illuminating. Speakers and writers should use short, lively words; eschew sesquipe-dalian verbosity.

You cannot learn well without listening and you can learn to listen well. A good listener is both tenderhearted and tough-minded. The tenderhearted listener gets the feel of a situation, is sensitive to the needs of others, builds emotional kinship. The tough-minded listener knows how to tell a fact from an opinion, is neither a slave to unrelated facts nor at the mercy of sweeping generalizations. A critical listener is a person with a good mind.

It is not hard to convince a person that critical thinking and reading are important. But we have not thought adequately about the role of listening as a factor in developing the good mind. Clearly you cannot develop a good mind unless you listen critically. It does not require rigorous research to prove that there is more talking in this world than listening. In *The Merchant of Venice*, Shakespeare had Gratiano say, "I am Sir Oracle, and when I ope my lips, let no dog bark!" But unin-terrupted speech may fall on deaf ears. The lecture fails to captivate, the sermon lulls, the discussion lags. Why don't we listen?

The answers are both simple and complicated. First, we don't listen if we can't hear. In a radio interview Alfred Lunt was once asked, "What do you think is the most important talent for an actor or actress to develop?" He said, "You know, Lynn and I have talked about this, and we agree that it's the ability to speak so that the person in the last balcony seat can hear."

Second, most discussions about listening ignore the fact that we all like to talk more than we like to listen. I remember a person who said, "It was a wonderful discussion. I talked three times." We have all heard of compulsive talkers, but did you ever hear of a compulsive listener? J. B. Priestly says, "It is the most shadowy play of vanity to arouse the interest of people in whom we are not prepared to interest ourselves."

Third, we don't listen because we are fed up. Too many people are firing too many different ideas at us. We can't absorb them that fast. A poor speaker covers 10 points. A good speaker uncovers one, and provides many examples, anecdotes, and occasional quips.

On this point Priestly says:

> Anecdotes are the condiments in talk—the most general forms of talk are apt to be either flat or rather grim without some seasoning of anecdotes. The stories themselves should be welcomed for their own sake, should be good enough to stand by themselves, if necessary. But at the same time they should be illustrative, apt and pointed, coming in easily to carry the talk forward.

Anecdotes also provide thinking space, give us time to reflect a little on what has been said.

People may listen *actively* or *marginally*. The marginal listener mishears and misquotes. No matter whether we are listening to a lecture or are participating in a group discussion, we ought to know what was said. When someone says the minister gave a wonderful talk this morning, we have learned not to embarrass him by asking, "What did he say?" How many people really listen to the Biblical text as it is being read from the pulpit? And how many people try to see the connection between the sermon and the text?

Finally, we don't listen because we don't *become involved*. The speaker isn't answering the questions we have at the front or the back of our minds. So our listening is marginal, not active—a background to a pleasant reverie. We remain passive spectators, eavesdroppers, uninvolved participants. Maybe this is all the speech deserves, but perhaps we may put too much of a burden on speakers. We can expect them to set off a spark, but shouldn't we bring the kindling? The responsible listener is responsive. He meets the speaker halfway and doesn't defy him to "make it interesting." On the other hand, the dull speaker usually excuses himself by saying, "They weren't interested," instead of the more likely reason, "I wasn't interesting."

A good listener has mastered some of the skills of a good reporter. A reporter approaches an expert with questions in mind—not the superficial, amateurish, hackneyed questions you sometimes hear on television interviews, but questions that have grown out of reading and study. We can test our reporting skill by noting whether the television or radio interviewers we are watching or listening to asked the questions we would have asked. And if they are able reporters, they will also ask questions that we were not wise enough to ask *this* time but may learn to ask *next* time. Critical listening elicits critical questioning.

The Good Mind Is Creative

Creativity is defined in two ways: First, it is seen as a personal rediscovery of what has already been discovered. Second, creativity produces something entirely "new."

But a good mind must do more than rediscover the already known; it must also *produce*. The product may be a poem, a new way to teach reading, a slow-growing hybrid grass, a new synthetic drug, or a new theory of personality development. The results might be of great or of limited significance.

In developing a good mind, therefore, we face a choice between rote, imitative reaction and creative interaction. Since imitative reaction is the chief characteristic of our schools and colleges, the resulting learning by rote will be inadequate for future needs. If we aren't creative, we will wake up some day and find ourselves in the buggy-whip business.

We must emphasize creative interaction in our schools because we cannot predict what a person will need to know in the twenty-first century, or even in the final years of this century. Today's older doctors spent much time learning about diphtheria, infantile paralysis, tuberculosis, and mastoiditis—all of which are now going or gone as critical diseases in medical education. Since you can't *train* for an unpredictable and changing future, you must *educate* for it. True, not all of our new programs will succeed, but the creative person has learned how to fail successfully. Indeed, the world needs more "successful failures."

Suppose we want to promote creativity in several fields of study. How do we go about it? How can we make more intelligent use of what we already know—creatively combine old elements to develop the new?

24

For example, how do you *read* creatively? Many students believe that the best way to master an assignment is to read it over and over again. But is it? The best evidence is that re-*thinking* a passage is often more productive in terms of time spent than re-reading it. The students who re-create as they re-read are reorganizing the material and putting it into their own filing systems, making it readily available for later use.

A Mental Filing System

The good mind can file, retrieve, and refile information with ease. How can we best file mentally what we have learned, and how can we get it out when we need it? The more systematically we file our ideas, the better we can retrieve them and discover new relationships. There is creativity in skillful classification.

The good mind thrives on novelty. Hence the conceptual development so necessary for developing the good mind is promoted by novel, fresh, creative approaches. One day an able kindergarten teacher said: "Today is Friday. Let's think about it. What are all the things that Friday means to you?" Here are some of the children's replies: "We don't eat meat on Friday. . . . It's called Friday because that's the day we fry fish. . . . It's the last school day of the week. . . . It's the day mother does her shopping. . . . It's the day after Thursday and the day before Saturday. . . . There is a Good Friday; is there a Bad Friday?"

How can the idea of creative thinking be applied to the various subject matter fields? It is not easy. For example, there has long been critical discussion as to whether you can teach a person to be a writer. John Ciardi said in the *Saturday Review* (December 15, 1956):

> The truly creative—whether in art, in science, or in philosophy—is always and precisely that which cannot be taught. And yet, though it seems paradoxical, creativity cannot spring from the untaught. Creativity is the imaginatively gifted recombination of old elements into new. And so, it may be seen that there is no real paradox. The elements of an invention or of a creation can be taught; but the creativity must be self-discovered and self-disciplined.

In short, the teacher can give some advice about where and how to get the kindling, but the learner must generate the creative spark that sets it afire.

What is involved when children think creatively in mathematics? First, they can discover that the number system itself is a creative invention. It does not have systematic names until we get to 13 (three-ten) where highly creative persons recognized the possibilities of a more systematic approach. Thirteen is followed by four-ten, five-ten, six-ten, etc.

What about the good mind in personal relationships? We envy but do not always imitate those persons who are unusually creative in this field. They exhibit those heartwarming nuances of taste and conduct which distinguish a truly gracious person from an ordinary one. We all remember with joy those insightful comments that creative teachers with extrasensitive perception wrote on our papers. The instructor saw us as a person, cared about what we said.

We need to take a fresh, inventive, creative look at the curricula of schools and colleges. Do schools and colleges develop the good mind? Do they help students develop a mental filing system? Do they emphasize *production*. It's clear that they are geared to "input" but not to "output." We spend too much time acquiring information (often for temporary purposes) and too little time in processing and reorganizing, in putting information to work. We are more concerned about reproducing knowledge than we are about producing it. We emphasize the duplication of knowledge but do too little with creative explication, implication, and application. We need more "learning *for* doing."

Let us suppose that we tried to set up a school environment to develop the good mind. What would it be like?

To create good minds requires high respect for the dignity and the importance of every student. We would avoid using schools and colleges to sort out people, to pick the "winners." We would pay greater attention to picking up the "losers."

A creative environment will provide increasing opportunity for exploring experiences and for decision making. We will remember that the unpredictable adds zest to living and learning. The good mind craves novelty. There would be a higher level of self-discipline, of dedication, and of personal responsibility for learning. The good life is not the soft life. The goal is the development of independent learners who have a zest for learning.

Openness to experience would be considered a critical goal of the curriculum. We shall cherish the opening of minds and shun the closing of minds. We shall try to unfreeze "frozen perceptions."

We shall look for administrators and supervisors who consider creative thinking an important goal of the school. And, indeed, we shall select them for *their* creativity. We will expect them to be deeply concerned about ways in which they can release the latent energies and the powers of those whom they supervise. They will not see teachers or students as interchangeable parts in a bureaucratic machine.

In developing the good mind we shall be less concerned about the well-rounded, excessively conformist "smoothie" and have greater concern for the slightly elliptical, occasionally abrasive personality. We shall avoid adjusting our students to a world that is dying and prepare them for a world that is waiting to be born.

To develop the good mind we must sharply increase the quality and variety of teaching materials, provide more nonverbal learning for its own sake and as a preparation for verbal learning. Much of our teaching materials today require high verbal proficiency, yet the creative persons are not necessarily the fluent verbalists. We may be neglecting potential painters, photographers, musicians, architects, and sociologists by failing to see the key role of nonverbal experience.

We shall try to make our students enough alike so that they can communicate with each other, yet different enough so that they will have something worth communicating. Can we press too hard for a creative approach to all problems? Certainly we don't want creative spelling. How much change can we stand? We should aim for an appropriate balance between the stability provided by current knowledge and the necessary creative flexibility. We should be aware, too, that some people can't live comfortably with tentativeness.

The good mind is basically optimistic, has confidence in the long-run improvement of the human condition. For most of his life, H. G. Wells was such an optimistic person, but in his last book, *Mind at the End of Its Tether*, he notes:

28

The writer sees the world as a jaded world devoid of recuperative power. In the past he has liked to think that Man could pull out of his entanglements and start a new creative phase of human living. In the face of our universal inadequacy, that optimism has given place to a stoical cynicism. . . . Ordinary man is at the end of his tether. Only a small, highly adaptable minority of the species can possibly survive. The rest will not trouble about it, finding such opiates and consolations as they have a mind for.

The problem is clear-cut: Can the school and college play a dramatically larger part in starting "a new creative phase of human living" and add a significant number of creative men and women to the present "small, highly adaptable minority"? Can we create the good minds needed to develop this small, highly adaptable minority?

Certainly to have a good mind is to be thoughtfully involved in the problems of our society, a concerned and active participant, not a disengaged spectator. The creativity of a good mind transforms pleasure into joy, entertainment into delight, listless apathy into dynamic living. The great tragedy in life is not death but never having lived. The creative person, on reviewing his life, can say with Virgil's Aeneas, "Many of these things I saw, And some of them I was."

Values and the Good Mind

A good mind has clarified its values, given them priorities. When we read of the fall and decline of a nation or a civilization, disturbing questions arise. During the critical years of decline did the leaders sense their lessened power and prestige, their increasing decadence, the "failure of nerve"? Or did they look about and say in prideful arrogance, "We never had it so good"?

What, then, are the stigmata, the discernible evidences of the decline of a society? The first place to look would be its values, the goals its members prize and give priority to, the activities to which they give their greatest energy, the best years of their lives. How can a nation tell when it has lost its sense of self-confidence, the once jaunty air of daring and pioneering, its concern for the "huddled masses yearning to be free"?

It is neither easy to collect such evidence nor to draw up a truthful balance sheet for a modern society or for a nation. But certainly it is rewarding, even if upsetting, to burn away the mists of fancy, stereotyped rhetoric that obscure a good look at the truth. Even though we do this clumsily and incompletely, the process is stimulating.

Is the following comment by newspaperman Emile Gauvreau valid today?

> I was now definitely a part of that strange race of people aptly described . . . as spending their lives doing work they detest to make money they don't want to buy things they don't need in order to impress people they dislike.

General Omar Bradley has said that "Ours is a world of nuclear giants nd ethical infants." He said this about 20 years ago. The situation has grown worse in these intervening years.

Bernice Fitz-Gibbon, formerly advertising and merchandising consultant for *Seventeen* magazine, commented as follows at a fashion clinic for the "back-to-school fashion concept": "Your fashion department is the wooing chamber. Get the teen-age fly to come into your parlor and little by little the web will be spun. Then when the girl marries you haven't lost a customer. You've gained a gold mine." Miss Fitz-Gibbon went on to call the teen-age girl "a woman with means" with "a passion for possession," and urged retailers to go after "the teen tycoons, not in the sweet by-and-by, but in the much sweeter now-and-now." What a bitter epitaph for a world in ruins: They had "a passion for possession!"

I have stated some weaknesses in our national and individual values. But to what positive, countervailing values have we given our allegiance? What widely held values still disclose our high national purposes?

We are committed to human dignity, to a sense of the worth and self-fulfillment of all persons. Our great system of common schools symbolizes our attempts at universal education and our commitment to this purpose.

Today our great need is for uncommon schools and colleges designed to develop creativity, innovation, humane ideals, the good mind. What we need are creative plans for the constant renewal of dynamic living on our planet and an indication of where each one of us fits into these plans. First we must decide whether to let the machine control us or be in control of the machine.

Nearly every large American city is being choked by traffic. Our mass methods of transportation, the railroad and the city bus systems, are starved financially.

Do we use television to promote our national purposes, to bring a sense of the reality of the world to our over 200 million citizens, to promote our national values? Or do we use it primarily for entertainment, for fantasy, for purposes detrimental to the building of an informed national consensus? The burning issue on television seems to be how to take the shun out of perspiration, to smell good rather than to be good. At dinner time we are badgered by advertisers to do something about our personal plumbing, our alimentary canal.

One person can't save the world, but with good planning and co-operation of others he could improve one small part of it. We can protest deceptive advertising, indecent super-violence on TV. We can praise excellence wherever it appears. Certainly, no one is stopping us from reading excellent newspapers, magazines, and books or discussing these experiences with our friends.

We can become more aware of media choices day by day. We can choose the artistic and avoid the banal. The good mind chooses by thoughtful analysis and in light of possible consequences.

To act responsibly we must commit ourselves to certain values. How much do we really want world law and order? Do we believe in world health? Do we want to rescue older people from lives of bitter solitude? Are we concerned about giving hope and a sense of personal value to the forgotten fourth of students who do not now graduate from high school and who are often unemployed? Do we really prize active participation in community, national, and international life, or do we fit Emile Gauvreau's description noted earlier?

Of two things we can be certain: First, we cannot invigorate our national purposes with the philosophy of "What's in it for me?" Perhaps, too, we might stop talking about the American image and discuss the American ideal. An image can only reflect what we now are; an ideal can illuminate what we want to be. Are we flourishing as a society or are we in decline? The French historian Ernest Renan gives us a standard for judging: "To have common glories in the past, a common will in the present, to have done great things together, to wish to do greater; these are the essential conditions which make up a people." And all of these standards require thinking people, people with good minds.

Thinking Critically

What is critical thinking anyway? It is thinking that has been systematically criticized. It is meeting a forked road situation without a neat, exact road map. Critical thinking is the kind of sustained thinking necessary to deal adequately with personal and social questions.

Nearly everybody is for critical thinking. College presidents speak of it as a key goal of collegiate education. Teachers are for the active, independent mind as opposed to the passive, dependent mind.

Many teachers are trying to develop more effective, more concerned, more able thinkers in the field of communication. This involves the communication of messages we write and read, speak and listen, visualize and observe. Each of these three dyadic approaches to communication can be done critically or thoughtlessly, actively or passively.

But thoughtless acceptance of media messages will certainly undermine the good mind and finally cause readers, listeners, and viewers to conclude that you can't believe anyone. Indeed, confidence in the credibility of messages from government, big business, or big media is low. Many persons have concluded that these messages are often dishonest and cite illustrations to "prove" their belief.

It is generally agreed that the good mind can 1) identify central issues, 2) recognize underlying assumptions, 3) evaluate evidence or authority, 4) draw warranted conclusions, 5) recognize stereotypes and clichés, 6) recognize bias and emotional factors in a presentation, 7) recognize valid data, 8) determine whether facts support a generalization.

Admittedly the thinking abilities here noted are not simple or easily achieved. Nevertheless, they have simple beginnings, and critical thinking can and must be an objective of the elementary and high school. For example, before the children in a sixth grade visited the historical museum they read the pamphlets written by archaeologists. They were able to make some sound inferences as to the way Indians lived 500 years ago—their food, housing, source of fire. Back in school the children pooled their facts and built some supportable generalizations.

What about critical, creative thinking in the high school English class? John C. Adler, then a teacher of English in Westport, Connecticut, wrote me that he was "trying to find a way to get the children to tap their springs of creativity and fluidity, and still keep within the bounds of the positive, the additive, and the useful." He says,

> I've begun to fumble about. I've said, for instance, to a class which is reading *Tale of Two Cities*, "Let's write a short character sketch of Lucy Manette." Groans. "We'll do it on the chalkboard; everybody chime in." Groans. "Relax." Someone pipes up, "A girl with blond hair." I write it on the board. "A girl who needs someone to help her."
>
> Ah! There's your thesis sentence! "Lucy Manette is a girl who needs someone to help her." Can you ask for more? And the rest follows— original, penetrating, full of imagery. It is their own—they aren't mouthing what they think should be said. The girl who needed someone to help her stimulated them to write originally because that area beginning somewhere one-half inch below the skull gave it to them, and coming from their *creative unconsciousness*, it was theirs. It stimulated them as no green-on-white beautifully typographed textbook can ever do.

Many opportunities exist for developing the good mind in reading. Indeed all reading includes the making of inferences not only as to the amount of weight to be given a particular word or phrase in a sentence, but also as to what the sentences themselves mean when put together in a paragraph. And when we apply what we have read to the solution of a problem, we face again a thinking situation.

Students need to experience the fact of highly variant interpretations of the same reading material. Probably few would read "the early bird catches the worm" with a worm's-eye view and thus conclude that

34

it is best to be a slug-a-bed. But we do know that many college students interpret "a rolling stone gathers no moss" as favorable advice to avoid being a mossback and to pick up a fine polish.

Let us ask a high school or college class to read "A Double Barreled Detective Story," by Mark Twain. It contains this paragraph:

> It was a crisp and spicy morning in early October. The lilacs and laburnum, lit with the glory fires of autumn, hung burning and flashing in the upper air, a fairy bridge provided by kind Nature for the wingless wild things that have their homes in the tree tops and would visit together; the larch and the pomegranate flung their purple and yellow flames in brilliant broad splashes along the slanting sweep of the woodland; the sensuous fragrance of innumerable deciduous flowers rose upon a swimming atmosphere; far in the empty sky a solitary oesophagus slept upon motionless wing; everywhere brooded stillness, serenity, and the peace of God.

Many college and graduate students finish that paragraph unaware that Mark Twain is spoofing.

Critical thinking will be improved if students in the junior and senior high schools develop some elementary competencies in statistics. They can do simple polls within the school itself and note the errors that may creep in when safeguards are not set up. They can learn that in controlled experiments with new drugs, cooperating doctors may not know whether they are administering real drugs or sugar pills.

Abler students can report on the polling methods used by Gallup and others and note the techniques used to get adequate samples of the adult population. They can evaluate the methods used to obtain data on television habits. They can learn that statistics are sometimes used the way a drunk uses a lamppost, for support rather than for illumination.

There are many statistical traps for the uncritical reader. It is said that the rich and poor both experience the same average amounts of cold weather but that the poor get theirs in the winter and the rich get theirs in the summer. You can drown in water that *averages* two feet in depth. An Ohio high school senior told a college interviewer that he was not in the upper half of his class but added helpfully, "You know there aren't as many in the upper half as there used to be."

If a critically minded student in the high school history class asked, "How do we know whether an event occurred the way the author described it?" he would be facing the question of historical evidence. How does a good historian act when he deals with an event in which he is personally involved? Lord Acton instructed contributors to the *Cambridge Modern History* to write as if they lived at 30° west longitude in the middle of the Atlantic Ocean. The critical thinker, like the historian, must make a conscious and stubborn effort to get at the truth.

Is logic enough? Does it meet all the needs of critical and creative thinking? Do our neat and supposedly logical arrangements for teaching subject matter always fit the varied outcomes we are seeking? Is it true, as Harold Lasswell notes in *Psychopathology and Politics*, that

> The ultimate paradox of logical thinking is that it is self-destroying when it is too sedulously cultivated. It asserts its own prerogatives by clamping down certain restrictive frames of reference upon the activity of the mind, and presently ends in impoverishing the activity which it purports to guide into creative channels. It becomes intolerant of the immediate, unanalyzed, primitive abundance of the mind, and by so doing destroys its own source.

The noted inventor Charles Kettering said it more pungently: "Logic enables you to go wrong systematically." Our classifications can become too tight, too neat, too rigid. And a good mind supplies a needed flexibility. Critical thinking thus helps us avoid becoming prisoners of our past perceptions. Men and societies that can bend won't break.

The Good Mind Is Flexible

For many years we have talked about education in a changing society but have done little to educate for uncertainty. Perhaps the best insurance we can offer for this uncertainty is the presence of a good mind. To develop a good mind the student must learn how to learn and develop a taste for learning. The world of tomorrow needs flexible individuals, intelligently mobile individuals, individuals who can land on their feet when their jobs become technologically obsolete, individuals who can cope with the unexpected.

As noted earlier, to educate for flexibility we must distinguish between training and education. To train is to emphasize fixed responses, to stress immediate goals to the neglect of long-term growth. To educate, however, is to foster limitless growth, lifelong learning, to develop the good mind.

Mark Twain's story about the cat is in order here. He said that a cat that jumps onto a hot stove will never jump on a hot stove again. Nor, he added, will she ever jump on a cold one. The cat can be trained but, contrary to what cat-lovers may say, cannot be educated.

The person educated for flexibility will see the world in a fresh, inventive way: Such a person is not chained to the immediate, the customary, the habitual, not dependent on someone else to plan the route and show how to get there. Such persons will chart their own course.

To develop the flexible person with the good mind we must favor those learning experiences that have high transfer value to varied life situations. We must learn how to teach skills, attitudes, and concepts so that they not only meet current needs but can be generalized to future needs as well.

Education for flexibility will certainly include guidance in the fine arts. If we accept Dewey's definition of art as "the intensification of the ordinary," then the teacher's task is to help learners turn the common place into the creative. Mel Strawn of Antioch College described this approach to learning as "a heightening of the individual's perceptual awareness, an intensification of his sense of form. He sees more and comprehends more of what he sees."

In Anne Morrow Lindbergh's book, *Hour of Gold, Hour of Lead. Diaries and Letters 1929-1932*, she says that "an experience was not finished until it was written or shared in conversation." She also makes the point that "truth that is locked up in the heart—or in a diary—is sterile." It must be given back to life so that "the hour of lead" may be transformed or transmuted into the hour of gold. The good mind is a sharing mind.

An inescapable element in education for flexibility is an attitude favorable to change. This is hard to develop. It requires faith in oneself and in the future. Insecure people dread change. They walk backwards into the future, clinging anxiously and defensively to the past.

Often such people think they don't amount to much. They do not accept themselves and consequently do not accept others. Thus they remain either negative or emotionally immature in their outlook toward the future. Lacking insight into their own feelings of inadequacy and unimportance, they shrink their world to meager and manageable proportions. They may wish to be more flexible, more open-minded, but they do not feel up to it.

What can the school and college do to build an attitude more favorable to unprejudiced examination of new ideas? Certainly they can and must develop the self-confidence of students, build them up with repeated success instead of constant failure. They can develop a group atmosphere friendly to and supportive of change. Schools and colleges can help students admire what is admirable, become acquainted with heroic men and women who changed the world. They can provide continuing guidance in how to become a real person, one who has faith in the future, who has a good mind of his own.

To meet the striking social changes of the future, continuing education is a necessity. Emerson put it this way: "The things taught in

colleges and schools are not an education but a means of education."
And Seneca noted that "You should keep on learning as long as you're ignorant."

The flexibly educated person knows that today's fact may be tomorrow's fallacy. He agrees with Alfred North Whitehead that "Knowledge does not keep any better than fish" and accepts his warning against "the aimless accumulation of precise knowledge, inert and unutilized."

The test of a modern society capable of meeting change with accelerated evolution instead of revolution does not lie in asking, "Is everybody happy?" but rather, "Is everybody learning?" To be learning is not only a condition for survival; it is also the basis for being richly alive.

A Good Mind Makes Good Choices

A person with a good mind is sensitively aware of the role of informed choice making in his or her life. Indeed, the range of choices, of options, is a major factor in the good life. If you restrict choices, you restrict the quality of living. One of the rewards of a good mind is this very opportunity to create and use choices. To develop a rich life you must optimize the options.

However, if an individual has no choice, or highly limited ones, if events are in charge, we have a stagnant society, a society eventually dominated by dictatorship.

Individuals who have real choices do make a difference. It is the informed choices of individuals that should concern us as we try to build a decent world. In a democracy the only way to safeguard choice is to keep choosing. In short, we might well define a good mind as one that makes informed choices. To choose wisely is to live well.

Harm can come to our society where freedom of choice is lessened. This is the danger of one-newspaper towns, of a one-sided press, of one-sided teaching, or of radio or television limited only to commercial stations. Danger may also arise when we mistakenly believe that no choices are open to us, that we are fenced in spiritually and intellectually.

The result can be to excuse ourselves from the responsibility of choice or from the discipline of making hard choices. The outcome might be either a cynical apathy or an irresponsible utopianism. We either think we can do nothing now or assume that everything will eventually come out all right without action on our part.

The choices of the good mind are informed choices, not random d thoughtless. The informed choice is also a free choice. A coerced noice is no choice at all.

The school and the home must note the choices that children and oung people are making and help make these choices wiser, better informed. Education comes at a point of choice. The appreciative or discriminating chooser is one who is sensitive to differences in worth or value. This sensitivity distinguishes the growing mind from the one hat is already stultified.

To choose wisely it is first necessary to have a wide range of choices, n easy access to excellence. There must be excellent books available n the classroom, the school library, the public library. There must be ooks that one can buy, reread, and react to by underlining or arguing with the author in the margins.

Schools and colleges have very real responsibilities for increasing he range and quality of choices. Further, it is not enough to provide a wide range of choice; there must also be guidance in the consequence of choice. Wisdom concerning consequences is what Dewey indicated was a characteristic of a good mind. Not only must someone in the schools speak for excellence, but such mentors must also be wise in ways of helping children and young people move toward increasing excellence in their daily choices. If we cannot improve today's choices, there is little likelihood that we are influencing tomorrow's choices.

Units in the teaching of discriminating choice should be included not only in the curriculum of teachers colleges but also in the social studies and English curriculum of the public schools. We strive to instill principles of discriminating choice in the field of literature, but little has been done to apply these same principles of discrimination to radio, motion pictures, and television as well.

To choose wisely is to receive the fruits of discriminating choice. It is to move away from the coercions of the crowd or the compulsions of the powerful. It means, in short, that we are on our own, that our tastes are growing up. Jean Paul Sartre said it well: "We are our choices."

Self-Discipline and the Good Mind

Self-discipline is the organization of one's time and talent to produce intended results. Without rigorous self-discipline a society degenerates, seeks excitement rather than enjoyment, makes pleasure a major goal, and defines success as getting ahead *of* other people instead of getting ahead *with* them.

Basic to all discipline is the habit of deferred gratification. There is a big difference, however, between the deferred gratification that comes from self-imposed discipline and that which is externally imposed. Deferred or postponed gratification is acceptable if the learner connects the means with the ends to be achieved. To lose sight of the goal is to lose the meaning of the self-imposed discipline. The meaning is in the means.

Further, civilized men and women set certain standards in regard to the nature of gratification. John Stuart Mill said, "It is better to be a human being dissatisfied than a pig satisfied; better to be Socrates dissatisfied than a fool satisfied."

The good mind requires the discipline of self-examination. Socrates said that the unexamined life is not worth living. Hence the good mind carefully examines purposes, values, goals. How do we now spend our time and energy? How do we use our options, our choices?

Many persons have trouble at this point. They find the present intolerable, the future fearful, and wish nostalgically to go home again where everything as they remember it was simple. Others reject the past, resent the present, and raise high hopes of a utopian future where "Every day is Sunday and Sunday is Christmas."

Obviously we cannot ignore the past or fail to plan for the future.

ut the discipline of living thoughtfully in the present makes the future tolerable and sometimes highly inviting. We must connect our past experience and our future hopes. By enlarging the meanings of the past and the future we can live in an expanded present. We must learn where we came from, where we are now, and where we are going. We are the sum total of all our experiences, good and bad. Our past and present experiences shape the things to come.

A second discipline required by the good mind is that of the guided practice that leads to competence. There is a big difference between talking about doing and an actual performance. Our output would be sharply raised if we decided after reflection to *do it now*. We are all aware that you do not become a highly competitive athlete, a painter, an actor, or a musician without rigorous practice. Yet we fail to see that this is true in all fields.

A disciplined person counts the cost of reaching a goal in terms of time, energy, money, and the things one must do without. Perhaps the most important of all disciplines is that of sharing. It cannot be learned without rigorous self-discipline. It is a mature ability, since it means that we must understand other people, get into their shoes, empathize. Sharing is a key ingredient in all communication. It means that one must be able imaginatively and creatively to exchange roles with another person. Sharing and caring go hand in hand. You can't share unless you care and you don't care unless you share.

For example, how do you explain or share with others what it means to live in the slums? How did it feel when you got the highest score on a qualifying test, but didn't get the job because you were black or a woman? Happily, in recent years this situation has been markedly improved.

What will be the need for disciplined activity in the future? Every generation in the United States until the 1900s faced the hard discipline of raising food, providing clothing and shelter. The farm furnished the inescapable discipline that comes from the regular caring for animals, the planting and harvesting of crops. There was a sense of continuity and purpose.

One was compelled by the situation to accept the discipline of farm chores. Every child was part of a cooperative enterprise where work

43

and play were shared. Today there are few such chores for boys and girls. Adjusting the thermostat is no substitute for splitting wood, firing the stove, taking out ashes. The unique discipline involved in milking a cow twice a day no longer prevails. Family duties may be prescribed, but they do not have the meaning of the adultlike chore performed on a farm. Today's "chores" may involve little more than doing one's homework, a necessary activity but not one in which the whole family usually shares.

Gunnar Myrdal, the distinguished sociologist, pointed out in *Asian Drama, an Inquiry into the Poverty of Nations* that the grave weakness of some underdeveloped countries is that they lack the self-discipline to make the best use of aid from developed countries. Societies usually are destroyed not because of danger from without but because of weaknesses within. To kill a society one needs only to reduce the opportunities for rigorous self-discipline.

The undisciplined view is illustrated in a fable by the Russian poet Krylov about a pig that ate his fill of acorns under an oak tree and then started to root around the tree. A crow sitting in the oak tree remarked, "You should not do this. If you lay bare the roots, the tree will wither and die." "Let it die," replied the pig. "Who cares as long as there are acorns?"

The disciplined view is illustrated in Arthur Koestler's *Age of Longing*, in which he has Monsieur Anatole say:

Do you know how long it took to make the Place de la Concorde into that miracle of landscape planning that it is? Three centuries, my friend. . . . To build perfection out of so much ugly detail, you must have a vision that embraces centuries, which digests the past and makes the future grow out of it; in other words, you must have continuity.

Summary

What then is the good mind? It is the whole mental faculty in action. It discerns, doubts, searches, probes. It answers questions and questions answers.

The good mind is critical. It asks, "What knowledge is of most worth?" and "How shall I spend the time of my life?" It deals with questions about the higher destiny of man, the problems of means and ends, and the specific questions of everyday life. The good mind communicates. It is compassionate and empathetic.

The good mind conceptualizes, sees relationships, makes connections, relates discrete facts, sees differences in similarities and similarities in differences. The good mind fuses specifics into generalizations. It is aware of specific facts and skills but visualizes them within the framework of an overarching design for learning.

The good mind knows the importance of nonverbal as well as verbal communication. It has an ear for music, an eye for art. It finds meaning in the intonation and pitch of a voice.

The good mind is tuned in to the speech of mankind. It listens with attention, speaks and writes with clarity and purpose. The good mind recognizes words as concepts, sees the need to give names to experiences so they can be shared.

The good mind knows how concepts develop, recognizes 1) the sensory appeal of the firsthand experience, the concrete event, 2) the semiconcrete experience of the picture or dramatization, and 3) the symbol of the event, the word. This symbolic representation is the highest concept on the concrete-to-abstract scale. The teacher helps students apply these concrete-to-abstract experiences to the higher mental processes of inferring, analyzing, interpreting, and synthesizing.

The good mind is creative. It produces something new, fresh, inventive, serendipitous. The good mind knows that only the creative society survives. The good mind embraces creative interaction. It anticipates what schools and colleges will need in the near and distant future.

The good mind looks closely at its values, its priorities. It considers the national and individual values and ideals. It is concerned with human dignity, and the self-concept of individuals. The good mind reexamines and retains the best of our national values.

The good mind is a critical mind, not carping or captious, but creative, evaluative, constructive. It is flexible. It makes good choices. It identifies issues, questions assumptions, and draws logical conclusions. It distinguishes fact from fallacy. The development of the critical mind should be a prime objective of the schools.

Critical reading is a major factor in developing critical thinking. It broadens experiences, provides opportunity for examining, comparing, inferring, judging. The critical mind applies what it reads.

Finally, a good mind is self-disciplined. It organizes time and energy to produce results. For the good mind pleasure is a circumstance, not a goal. The good mind postpones gratification for a higher ideal but seeks an attainable objective. It weighs its values and its goals. The good mind examines itself.

The good mind thoughtfully uses the past in planning for the future. The good mind wishes but it also wills. It practices self-discipline until it becomes habitual.

The self-disciplined person knows the importance of sharing—the prime factor in communication. A sharing person is a caring person. He or she respects, understands, empathizes, communicates. Rigorous self-discipline is the key ingredient in developing a good mind and building a civil society.

Daniel H. Burnham (1846-1912), an architect, once said,

Make no little plans; they have no magic to stir men's blood and probably themselves will not be realized. Make big plans; aim high in hope and work, remembering that a noble, logical diagram once recorded will never die, but long after we are gone will be a living thing. . . . Remember that our sons and grandsons are going to do things that would stagger us. . . .